Zero Point Soldier

Moshumee T. Dewoo

Langaa Research & Publishing CIG
Mankon, Bamenda

Publisher:
Langaa RPCIG
Langaa Research & Publishing Common Initiative Group
P.O. Box 902 Mankon
Bamenda
North West Region
Cameroon
Langaagrp@gmail.com
www.langaa-rpcig.net

Distributed in and outside N. America by African Books Collective
orders@africanbookscollective.com
www.africanbookscollective.com

ISBN-10: 9956-550-43-4

ISBN-13: 978-9956-550-43-2

Table of Contents

Preface

It took two years for this collection of poems to see the light of day. Two years. Two whole years. But two whole years of thinking, feeling and working through and from one of the strangest and certainly most torturous facts of life on Earth, and one of the least explored themes in the world of the modern woman of Africa, or my world, at least. This is the fact of Death. But not the fact of the death of all. Not the fact of the death of any. It is that of the modern man, the man, of Africa. And it is specifically about how the woman – a mother, a sister, a cousin, an ex-girlfriend, or just a friend who happens to be a girl, a concubine, a life partner, a wife, a niece… any woman in the life of this man… any woman who would have been in his life – who would have desired, liked or loved him in her own manner at some point, lives through his death and evolves beyond his absence. It is about her feelings then. It is about her. It is about her losing him. It is about her losing a part of herself. It is about her without his love, without his body… his voice… It is about her at zero point, when she must wake to him no longer existing. But it is also about her soldiering on therefrom. Because she can. Because she has to. Because she eventually does. And if it took two years to pen, it is because it took two years to understand.

1. The Taste of Grey

Once was blue
And twice was not
A story of hue
'Round things that rot

A tale so pale
A blackened end
One life on scale
A bitter friend

A girl in grey
Her stone in veil
For night to prey
In cloak on sail

One promise made
To dust and sky
The hand betrayed
One tear too shy

Hear this rhyme, I call
To eyes unwise
Beware her fall
And all goodbyes

Because, old heart
She killed once more
I died, old heart
She lied once more
And you know what, old heart?
Oh?

You want to know?
Well, this rhyme, old heart, is but big show!

And you can go to hell, old heart
Yes, you too can go!!!
I did pray for you, sweetheart
It was murder slow

2. God is Dead

God is dead
He said
Man is free
Forever
Forgiven
Forgotten
Maybe
But what about her?
And me?
Poor me
God is dead
What about me?
Tell me!
What will now be?
God is dead
He said
But that is not true!
God is gone!
God left me
She said
Through the door on the right
He ran
Out of time, sadly
Out of line
Not a word was heard
Not one whisper spared

God is dead
He might as well be
Or is he a she?
God is dead

She said
She might as well be
Sent to hell

Guilty

God

God

Guilty

3. Tender the Man

Tender the man
Who comes this night
To ask for your hand
And beg for no fight
Tender the man
Gentle his grin
Slender he stands
In Hamelin
Wait!
Hush, now!
Hear!
Hear the brothers scream
"Grim,
Grim,
It is him!"
Oh! No!
Old friend
Indeed
It is him
He, who lures pest on whim
Do not follow
Do not go
I beg you
Do not give in

4. Lady River

Lady River
Had a lover
A man of hate
One man made bone
Alone
Who
Too
When
Tired his shoe
Sang to three
And four
Only to be no more
Like so
Five
Never was six
Since
Lady Lover
Down the river
Would drown
By the Scripture
The good man
Never the preacher

5. Make me Better

Bite my tongue
By the tide
Bind me whole
Burn your wild
Watch me wake
Your silence
Your patience
Running mild
On your neck
Your kingdom
Your anger
Commander
Is full crown
For the clown
And the Crow
In the crowd
Now unbowed

On my tongue

For how long?

For how long
Will it long
By the tide?

6. Choo Choo no Wagon

My little boy blue
You, insane and pale
You, without eyes
You, without a clue
You like the train
And fairy tales
Don't you?
And hands of hail,
Cold hands too?
You chase them all
I see you
"Choo choo", you go
Winding off track
On sugar low
I see you
Poor little you
My poor little boy blue
You, who have paid your due
Here, hold my hand
It is old, just like you want it
Like you like it
Like you love it
Love
Screaming
Freezing
Bold
Let us go
Let me take you to the train
Track
My step
My glow

My feet, soft, into your shadow
How they melt toward each other
Fierce little boy
My little boy blue
Boy without a damn clue
You have well paid your peace
Your malfeasance too
Haven't you?
Come on, now
Little sparrow
We must go

Clock

Clock

You must let go

7. The Spaces that Haunt

Do not cry for me, mother
When you find bits of me
Dancing their last dance
Do not cry when you see the dear damned
Sipping on the last drops of my blood

Drips

Thrips

On my lips
On my pain
My grief
My strife
My all, my nothing

Do not fear for me, mother
Do not be afraid of the day I leave
Do not be afraid of the sacred inside of me
Inside of you
Do not close your heart to infinity and endlessness

Ease

Please

Remember, instead, mother
That I was born of you
I am you
I am the child of all that is true
Part him, part clue

I am not weak, mother, unlike you
I can face the end
The end of you and me
And him and me
The end of all in me

8. Coco Java

I asked for a little more time
A few more days
A little praise
A bruise, but not a big one
A cruise
The ocean breeze
The sun on my skin

Setting

Settling

I asked for one more sin
Another morning
A little more warmth
A little love
From the noble belle
The sugarcane dove
The scent of molasses
The sweet coco

Coffee

9. Sand Lines

You taught me
The language of the sand
Born of the gods
Carved in the land
Crisp
Dry
Strong
Burning
Whimsical
Eternal

Light

It is the language of you
Too
I pen you today
In everything that I do
In everything that I hear
In everything that I live through

10. I Miss You

I think
I think
I think
I think
And I think
And I think
And I think
And I think without ever stopping
I think too much
I think that I think too much
I know that I think too much
And then I drink
To stop thinking
But I drink too much
One more glass
One last sip

Too much

And then I think about my drinking
I do not leave the house
I do not leave my bedroom
I do not like people
I hate my friends
I do not want to see them
There is nothing that I want to do but drink and stop
thinking
There is nothing else to do
There is nothing more to do
There is nothing to do without you
There is no me
When there is no you

11. The Happily Dead

And what if I must go to the pyre
Before does my father?
It will relieve me of my flesh

Dirty

It will cleanse me
Of the thousand reasons that you had
To keep me

I was not promised to you

So, let me go
Let go of me
Let me leave
I cannot care
I no longer care
Throw me out
Feet first
Or not!
I do not care!
Cover the mirrors
And then let me burn
Smear the windows with my ashes
Let me be free
I cannot care
I no longer care

12. 3 a.m. Vagary

3 a.m.
Spring
Melody
I break on repeat
Bone to bone
Until I fall asleep

13. Loser takes All

Master of all dark things
Master of broken hearts
Master of knotted strings
Yes, of course!
I am terrified of you
You can break me
You will break me too

Violently

Or gently, if you have had a good day
Well, that has never quite happened before
And I am not lucky anyway

So, it will be violently

But know
That I will fight you when you show
I will fight you at point zero

14. The Right Burial and the Wrong

I spent years under the moon
Grazing the path to my pen
Hoping for a final letter to you
I thought of kind quotes that did not carry forever
I obsessed over words that would last beyond my anger

I liked none

I wrote none

15. Asraar

It would break into a million pieces
That heart of yours
Over the red piano, too big for your hands
The Stephen King books that your mother would buy
reluctantly, thinking that they could be too scary for you, and
which your idiot of a little cousin would scribble all over
They would be worthless at that point
The bird that your dog would eat by the front porch
Where was its mother?
And father?
Would they not miss their child?
You thought that they would, and it would make you cry
A horror show!
Then, the wound on your face that you knew would leave a
scar
It would
It did
You thought that you would no longer be beautiful
But you would be
You were
You still are, even with your scar
Especially with your scar
The ice cream truck too, that would not come although it was
a Sunday
And it would always come on Sunday!!!
Aaaaaaaarrrgh!!!
Your grandmother would make a pie that day
And your grandfather would read the newspaper with you
To you
For you
So, you would be okay

A boy in high school for whom your heart would race
But he could not care if you existed
You were quite sure that he did not know that you existed
A friend hanged
A hanged friend
A friend lost
A lost friend
A rejected job application, which would matter little, really
Because you would find better anyway
Because you always found better anyway
The red piano would turn into concert nights
To hell, with King and the scribbles!
You would write your own books
Your ears would always turn to the chirping birds, easing you
off into the heaviness of a long day
You would fall in love with a boy with a scar
A beautiful boy
A magical boy
And he would love you
And he would love your scar
You would learn to make ice cream, and would try hard at
some frozen yogurt too!
You would no longer wait for Sunday
You would miss your grandmother's pie
But you would be okay
You would be okay
Because, although it would break into a million pieces,
That heart of yours would also be your little secret
Your *asraar*
Your hope kept

16. La Calma

We flow like electricity
Searching
Through the roots of trees
Searching
Dancing in every drop of rain
Searching
In every beam of sunlight
Searching
We are the cracks of lightning
My darling
Like the sound of ruffling leaves
We run on wind
Searching
Like the atoms in a molecule
And the nerves in the inside out brain
Searching

17. Wolf in Wave

Wolf of the East
Wolf a Star
Wolf once Man
Walking on four
Your path is pure
I have seen it
I have seen you
I have watched you
Heart in hand
War on land
Leap
To Woman
To guard
To guide

Her

Devil

You are born to kill
For the soul of Medine
The spirit of Medicine

18. Looking Glass

Many a year ago
In a land by the sea
I met a boy who liked to play
Hide
And then
Seek
I watched him
Backward
My knees all too weak
My faith too
My power, gone
None
I had fallen
Not an angel
More a demon
A dragon, baby!

19 Death by Nutella

"Where were you hiding?" he asked.
"I was not", she said. "I was lost."

Oh! A masterpiece!!!
A lugubrious melodrama…
Sweetness overdose
A love story in Africa

20. Three Fake Free

3 am
Again
The bird sings
Again
I am cut
Again
All pierced through
Again
I bleed words
Again
I scream tears
Again
My eyes shut
Again
My soul sinks
Again
You are dead
Again
I smell dope
Again
I am up
Again
3 am
Again

21. Awake?

Here I am
Lost once more
Between night and day

Can I ever dream?
Or must you try so hard at keeping me awake?

22. Good Hope, Bad Faith

The devil is at it again
He sent you to me, did he not?
Tell me the truth!
He sent you!
You, you, so perfectly you. So magnificently you…
And he watches.
He waits.
He grins as I continuously, endlessly, madly, erratically drown
in love with you
You, you, so perfectly you. So ethereally you…
He is playing with me again, is he not?
He is at it again, is he not?
He has been trying to rip what is left of my heart
And he will
He will
If he takes you away
He will
When he takes you away

23. 08/08

I read the other day
That, when wounds are healed by love
The scars can only be beautiful

Mine are ugly

24. Higher

There are poems too long
They drag out
They drag me along

There are poems too short
And like this one, perhaps,
I feel a little tired

25. Are You Ready?

Doubt my words
My hands
My mouth
Feathers
The sun
And my feet too
But, please, not my heart
Not my heart
It is a home
A house
A storm, sometimes
But a home
My home

It is art
My art
Content, at last

26. Aslan

I made a new friend
He does not talk to me much
He roars
He never wants to kiss me
He bites
I like it
I like him
Then again…I am a little gauche
A little self-absorbed
Graceless
You know that
And sometimes I hurt him
I cut him

But his wounds… they bleed rose petals, my love!
Flowers!

27. God (verdomme)

He does not have witchcraft on his lips!
He has honey
Fever *sans* fire
Desire
Ropes and shackles
Mistakes and misfortunes
Midnight conversations
Short and troublesome
Jewels and books
Duels and sins
Spirits and danger
Blades and flames
Earthquakes, wild things
Quiet tones
Of marble and stone
Bones
Pine cones and toffee
For thieves
With four leaves
And starlit ears
At pity parties
Smoke… Tears…
Prisons and rib cages
A ritual
All rituals
Olden cities
And Saint Peter
Not witchcraft!
Not witchcraft, Shakespeare!

28. ¡Quiereme! times three

Now
I am not I
Or me or eye
You see
I was
In the morning
But no longer
Do I need to be

Now
I am not I
Or sea or sky
You see
I was
In the morning
But no longer
Do I want to be

Now
I am not I
Or bee or fly
You see
I was
In the morning
But no longer
Can I be

29. Magie *sans* toi

There is a scream
A metaphor
In the forest
Of gold and ore
It is present
But not always
Except for those
Who guard blue jays
It plays on drums
On the other side
And inhales winds
To save tongue dried
It makes space grow
Between nothing
That all dream of
As thought waiting
It wants the dead
It owns the soul
One foot in sand
The other whole

This is the scream
Of carnivore
A forest spelled
A shift at core

30. Chariot

It gets better
I am told
It must get better…
The long, sleepless nights
They should be easier
Gentler
Soon
Soon, I am told
But I should eat first
I am told
I should get some sun
I am told
I should write something in a book
I should write a book
I should write about you
I should write something
I should do something
Anything
I should
I should
I should…
They all know better
That it gets better
That it will all be better
That I will feel better
Soon
Soon, I am told
And I go along
I play along
I act a little fragile
A little cold

I try a tear
I cry old pain
Because this,
This is not new
This is nothing new
Because this,
This is not as bad as they think
I do not feel as bad as they think
That you left
That you died
That you are corpse
At this point in my life
Because you were corpse in my life
Long before you left
Long before you died
Because I know of sleepless nights
And I love them more than I probably should
More than I dare show
And I know not of hunger
Well, I do…
It keeps me a size zero
And I know not of the sun
Or need it on my skin
What good is it anyway?
When I can lose myself in the clouds
Drown in the rain
To die
And wake again
And that, that, love, is what I would write in a book!
That is what I should write a book about!
Because you were corpse in my life
Long before your body left
Long before your body died

Because, love, I do not have it me to think of you
And not feel you
To mourn you
Dead
Because, love,
You died long before you left
Long before you died
Long before you were corpse in my life
Because, love,
I died long before you left
Long before you died
Long before you were corpse in my life

31. Taa'na

Three ghosts in dark
Knocked at my heart
On one sunny day
To tell me that the only way back home
Was to see, first, that there was no way back
And then, that there was no home at all

32. Pixie

I had a bag
Full of dust

Pixie

I was once a fairy
You see
But I threw my bag away
One night
It must have been too heavy to carry
Or did I think, maybe, that I would not need it
Like I do this day?

33. Darling and Ever

You do not read my poems anymore

34. Point of no Return

If I am not master of my sound
Am I work in progress?
Or, am I bound?

35. Nature

I am not saint
Stop calling me one
I am stillness
Madness

A world

Divine

36. Control

I knew all of it
All of you
I chose all of it
All of you

Nothing true

37. Time

It is late
God has not shown
Neither have you

I am bored
And I am getting old

38. Idyll

He promised you
Sunshine
And rainbows
In your mind

He told you stories
None of which he left behind

39. Sensible Intention

The tick tock
Of my soul
Petrified
And breathless
Prays 'fore
The cuckoo's clock
That you approve my hand
Now
Senseless

40. As so went the Flo(w)

After you
Came silence
Broken
By a man played on a piano
A medicine man
An architect of the mind
No less
By the name of Flo
Whose body was a bird
Tangled in my hair
Like scandal old
A tale not of Earth
Tattle never told before
About a girl
Who could break temple
Hand and gore

Printed in the United States
By Bookmasters